Series Editors
JOAN KANG SHIN & JOANN (JODI) CRANDALL

Authors
JILL KOREY O'SULLIVAN & JOAN KANG SHIN

UNIT 0	LET'S SHARE!	2
UNIT 1	STAND UP, SIT DOWN	6
UNIT 2	IT'S RAINING	14
UNIT 3	WILD ANIMALS	22
UNIT 4	SINGING AND DANCING	30
UNIT 5	SEE, SMELL, HEAR	38
UNIT 6	STORY TIME	46
UNIT 7	IT'S A PARTY!	54
UNIT 8	OUR WORLD	62
PROJECTS		70
THE ALPHABET		78
I CAN...		80
PUPPETS		
STICKERS		

Australia • Brazil • Mexico • Singapore • United Kingdom • United States

TOUCH

READ

COUNT

WRITE

DRAW

COLOR

VOCABULARY PRESENTATION **7**

8 VOCABULARY PRACTICE / PREWRITING

EQUALS

12 CONTENT CONCEPTS PRACTICE

REVIEW / SPEAK

2 IT'S RAINING

RAINING — AN UMBRELLA

WINDY

CLOUDY

SUNNY — SUNGLASSES

SNOWING — MITTENS

VOCABULARY PRESENTATION 15

16 VOCABULARY PRACTICE / PREWRITING

3 WILD ANIMALS

24 VOCABULARY PRACTICE / PREWRITING

4 SINGING AND DANCING

SINGING

CLAPPING

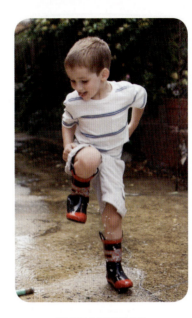
STOMPING

A DRUM

A GUITAR

DANCING

SHOUTING

A PIANO

VOCABULARY PRESENTATION 31

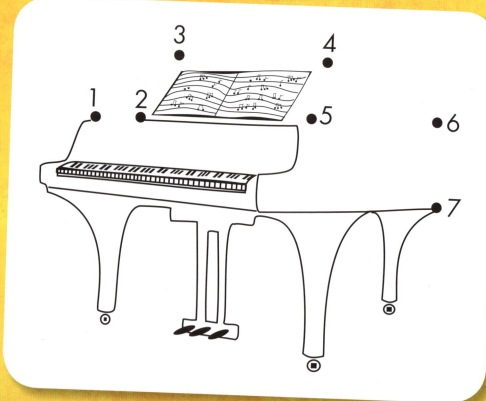

32 VOCABULARY PRACTICE / PREWRITING

SONG 33

36 CONTENT CONCEPTS PRACTICE

5 SEE, SMELL, HEAR

EAT

SEE

SMELL

FEEL

DRINK

HEAR

TASTE

VOCABULARY PRESENTATION 39

40 VOCABULARY PRACTICE / PREWRITING

SONG 41

6 STORY TIME

A CASTLE

A KING **A QUEEN** **A PRINCESS** **A KNIGHT**

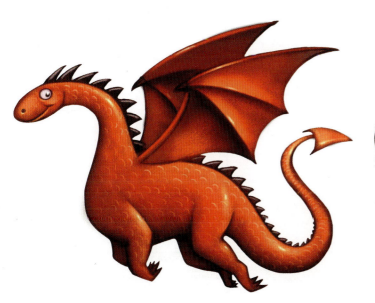

A DRAGON **A GIANT** **A TREASURE**

VOCABULARY PRESENTATION

48 VOCABULARY PRACTICE / PREWRITING

7 IT'S A PARTY!

56 VOCABULARY PRACTICE / PREWRITING

SONG 57

8 OUR WORLD

A CLOUD

A MOUNTAIN

A BRIDGE

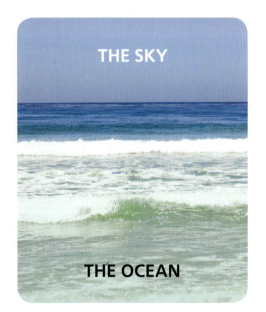

THE SKY

THE OCEAN

A RIVER

A ROAD

VOCABULARY PRESENTATION **63**

64 VOCABULARY PRACTICE / PREWRITING

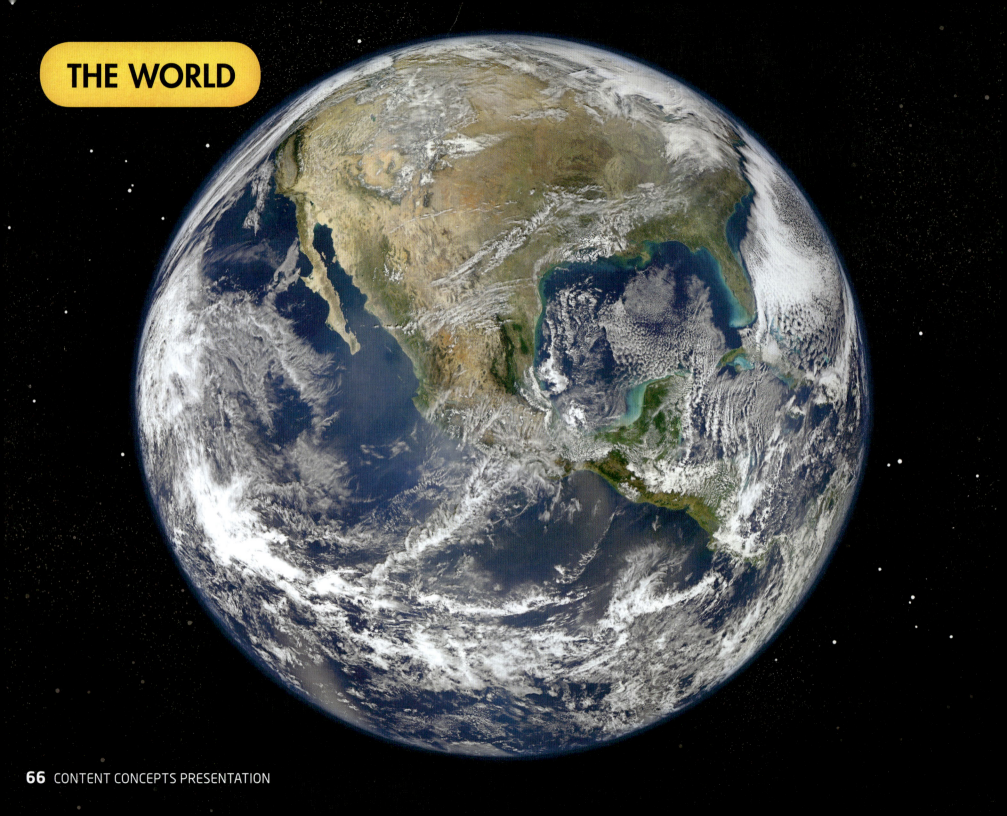

THE WORLD

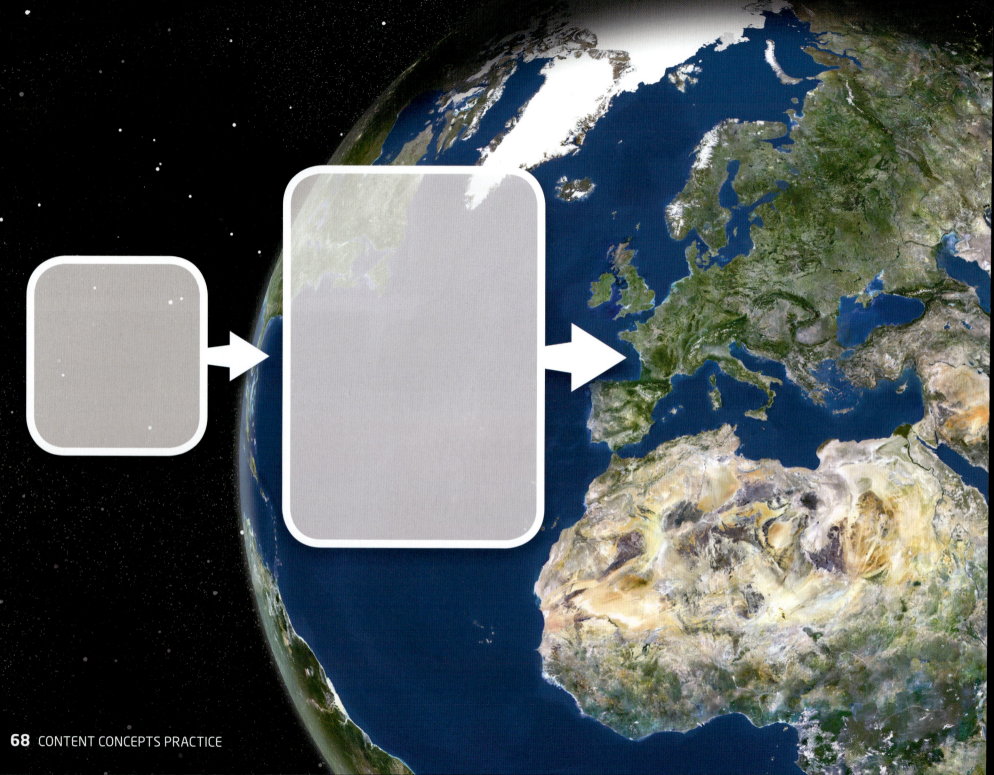

1 MAKE A COUNTING SPIDER.

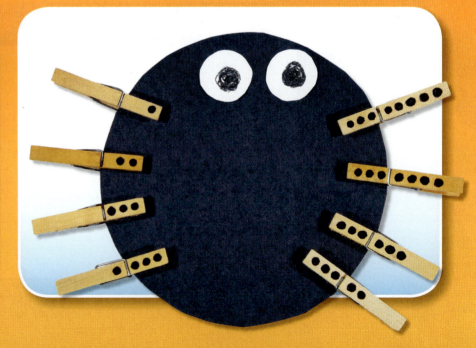

70 PROJECT

2 MAKE A RAINY DAY SCENE.

3 MAKE A PENGUIN.

72 PROJECT

4 MAKE A DRUM.

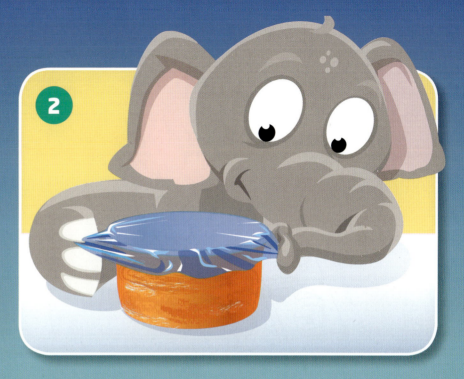

5 MAKE A FIVE SENSES POSTER.

6 MAKE A DRAGON.

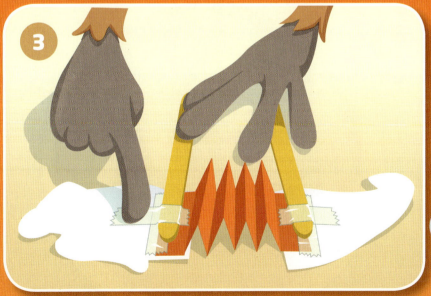
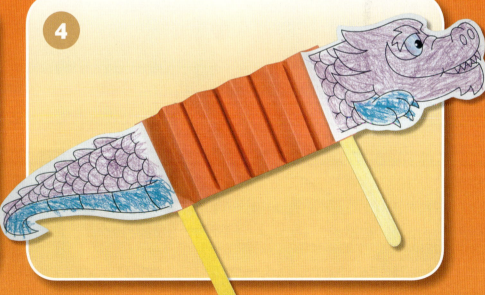

7 MAKE A PIZZA.

8 MAKE A GLOBE.

PROJECT 77

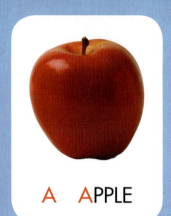 A APPLE

 B BUG

 C COOKIE

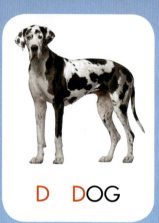 D DOG

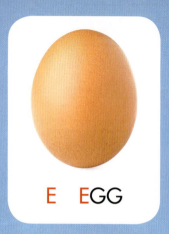 E EGG

 J JUICE

 K KING

 L LION

 M MILK

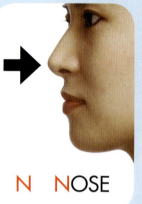 N NOSE

 S SOCKS

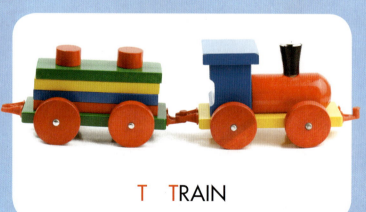 T TRAIN

 U UMBRELLA

 V VIOLIN

THE ALPHABET

F FIRE TRUCK

G GOAT

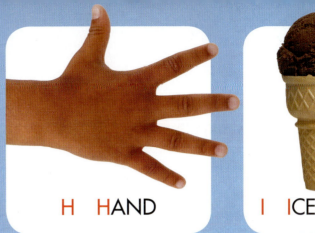
H HAND

I ICE CREAM

O ORANGE

P PUZZLE

Q QUEEN

R RABBIT

W WINDOW

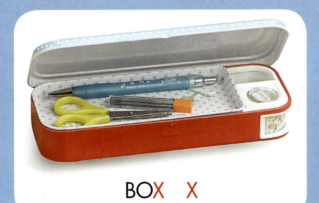
BOX X

Y YOGURT

Z ZEBRA

THE ALPHABET 79

1 I CAN TALK ABOUT MY CLASSROOM.

2 I CAN TALK ABOUT THE WEATHER.

3 I CAN TALK ABOUT WILD ANIMALS.

4 I CAN TALK ABOUT MUSIC.

5 I CAN TALK ABOUT FEELINGS.

6 I CAN TALK ABOUT STORIES.

7 I CAN TALK ABOUT PARTIES.

8 I CAN TALK ABOUT MY WORLD.

2 IT'S RAINING STICKERS

1 STAND UP, SIT DOWN STICKERS

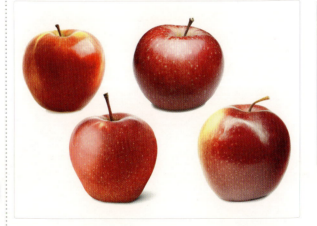

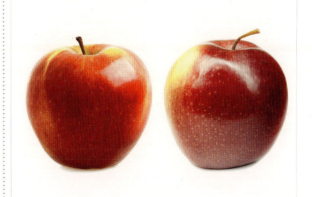

6 STORY TIME STICKERS

| 1 | 2 | 3 |

5 SEE, SMELL, HEAR STICKERS

8 OUR WORLD STICKERS

7 IT'S A PARTY! STICKERS

4 SINGING AND DANCING STICKERS

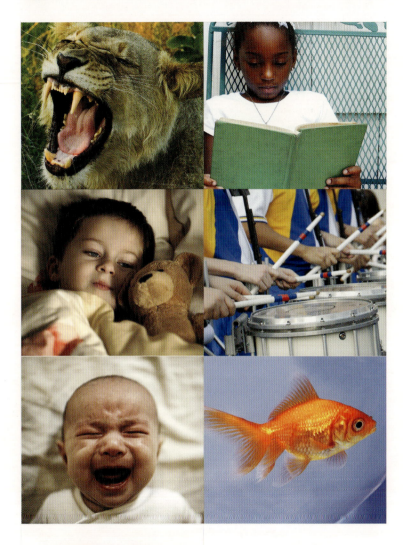

3 WILD ANIMALS STICKERS